Route 66 Races

"Competition is about inspiring each other
to apply our potential for the better of all."
-Doug H. Knutson

The Parts

In this fifth volume of the series, we will cover
the topic of parts and some maintenance.

The basic parts used or included with the cars
are as follows:

Chassis, Axles, Axle Gears, Counter Gears,
Bearings, Bearing Sleeves where applicable,
Wheels, Tires, Battery Switch, Battery Terminals,
Motor, Motor Mounts, Pinion Gears, Motor
Cover, Brakes and Spoilers aka Transponder
Mount Assembly, Spacers, Screws and Washers,
Rollers, Plates, Bodies, Front and Rear Body
Latches.

preface

The Chassis

The main part of the car is the chassis, upon and within which all other parts are attached.

Each driver may only have one chassis per race.

If a chassis is damaged during a race, the driver may have several options for choosing how to repair that chassis in order for the car to be able to continue in that particular race.

Bear in mind that the repaired chassis must be deemed safe by a marshal before re-entry into the race.

Any chassis repair or other repair that continues to break during a particular race may earn the car a black flag, ending the day for that car.

The Axles

Axles should be straight in shape straight out of the box, however, some are bent when new.

There are axle checker tools that help check for the slightest bend that may not be able to be seen with the human eye.

A bent axle will result in inefficiency of power transfer from the wheel to the axle gear.

The axle gear may become damaged by the undulation between the itself and the counter gear connecting to the pinion gear which is mounted on the motor shaft.

Additionally, the tires will have uneven rotation resulting in a porpoising effect or wheel bounce.

Bent axles may be a rare occurrence, yet it is always a good pit crew that has a straight one on hand.

2

The Axles Gears

The axle gear is mounted on the axle and transfers energy from the axle to the counter gear which in turn transfers energy to the pinion gear which is itself mounted on the motor shaft.

As previously mentioned, the axle gear may become damaged by the undulation of a bent axle by causing a cycle of loose slippage and over tightness against the counter gear.

Slippage and over-tightness will result in wear on the axle gear teeth and counter gear teeth and will eventually strip those gear teeth.

Striped gear teeth will result in reduced to zero energy being transfered from the motor to the tires.

The Bearings

Mounted between the axle and the chassis, the bearings provide a reduced friction environment allowing for faster rotation resulting in faster speeds.

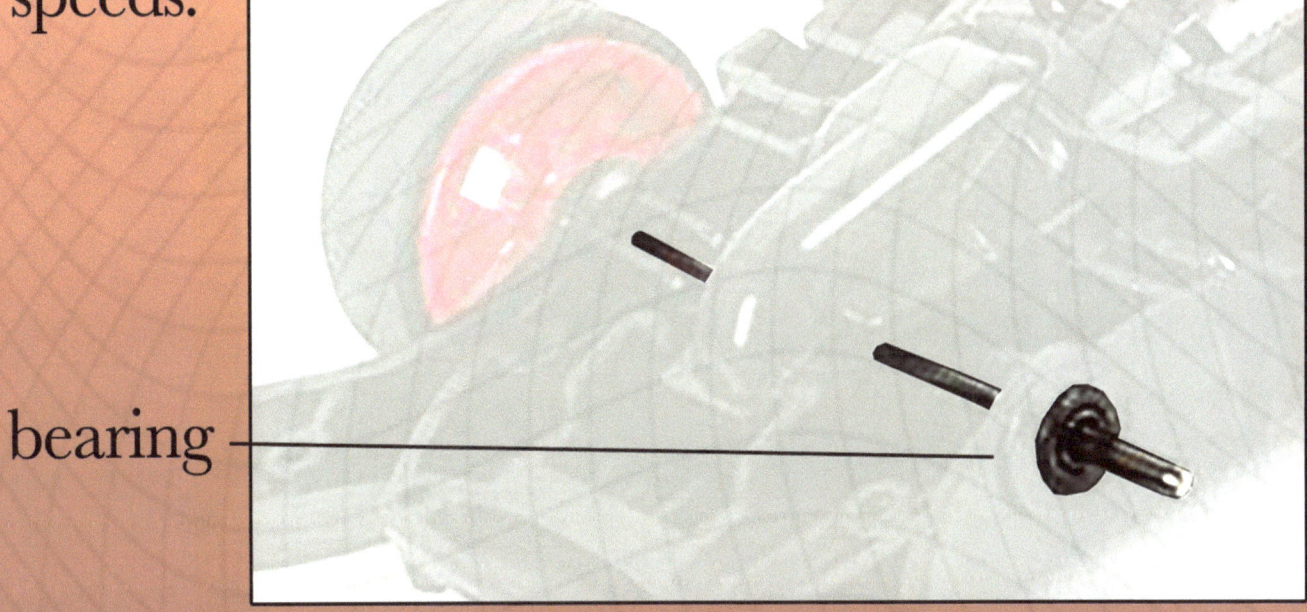

bearing

There are plastic bearings with brass sleeves that will wear down and need to be replaced. Other plastic bearings without brass sleeves last longer.

Metal bearings provide greatly reduced friction and last longer, yet will seize up if not properly maintained with the appropriate oils.

ROUTE 66 Races

The Counter Gears

Another step in the energy transfer from the motor to the tires is the counter gear.

counter gear —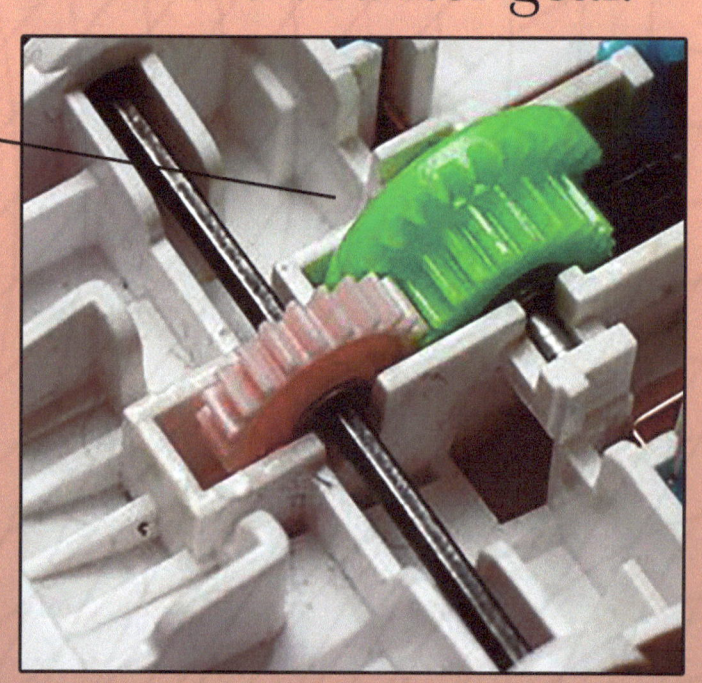

Counter gears are located between the axle gear and the pinion gear of the motor and come in a variety of ratios.

Since the counter gears are made of plastic, the teeth will wear down over time.

Counter gears have their own axles and bearings.

For counter gear bearings, some are made of plastic and others are the metal ball bearing type, yet either way, it is always a great idea to have a spare set.

5

The Wheels

There are many styles of wheels available, yet for the purpose of identification, we have certain wheels that qualify for use in particular speed classes.

HY, LMP2 , LMP3

GT2

GT 3, GT 4

TCR

ROUTE
66
Races

The Wheels (continued)

Plastic is soft and is prone to deform which could result in a wheel not rolling straight.

The benefit of plastic wheels is that they are lightweight and easily replaced.

Other wheels, made of aluminum are more heavy and although they do not deform, they are still attached to the axle with a plastic sleeve which, itself, is susceptible to deformation.

It is important to remember, that many factors are at play in which wheel is best since a plastic wheel may provide more shock absorption and its lower weight will allow more speed, however, the weight and stiff ride of aluminum wheels might be tactical.

The Tires

After tires are mounted onto their wheels, the outer diameter may be between 24mm* and 27mm* which is limited by the wheel well of the car body.

The actual thickness of the tire, itself, may be from 1mm to 3mm whether it has been trimmed or is at the unaltered, default thickness.

Tires may be made of soft or hard rubber.

Wheel tape is allowed for keeping tires from separating from the wheel at higher speeds.

*each 0.1mm can add 133+ meters traveled in a 2-hour race.

ROUTE 66 Races

Batteries Switch and Terminals

Energy flows from the batteries through thin, flat bands of copper coated zinc with the similar function to wires.

These bands are called "terminals" and are also available with a "gold" coating.

When the battery switch is in the "closed" circuit position, the energy is allowed to flow and the car is then considered to be "on" and ready to race.

Due to the rough nature of racing, the battery terminal could use a bit of support in the form of tiny sponges inserted behind the battery contact areas.

9

The Motor

Depending on the chassis, the motor either sits in the front, middle or rear and transfers the energy from the battery terminals to the pinion gears.

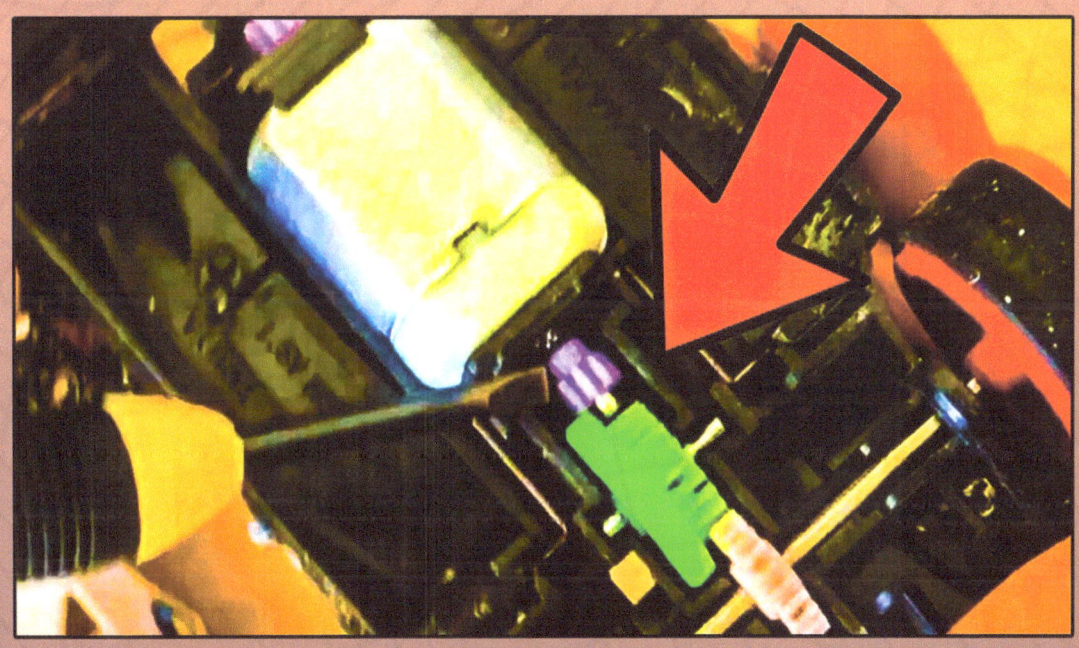

For endurance racing, brushed motors only last about 2.5 to 3.5 hours before they quit working, which is long enough to complete a 2-hour race.

In another volume, we will discuss "coreless" motors that last hundreds of hours.

ROUTE 66 Races

The Pinion Gear

Here, in the same image, we can see the pinion gear as the purple item that is affixed to the motor shaft located between the motor and the counter gear which is colored green.

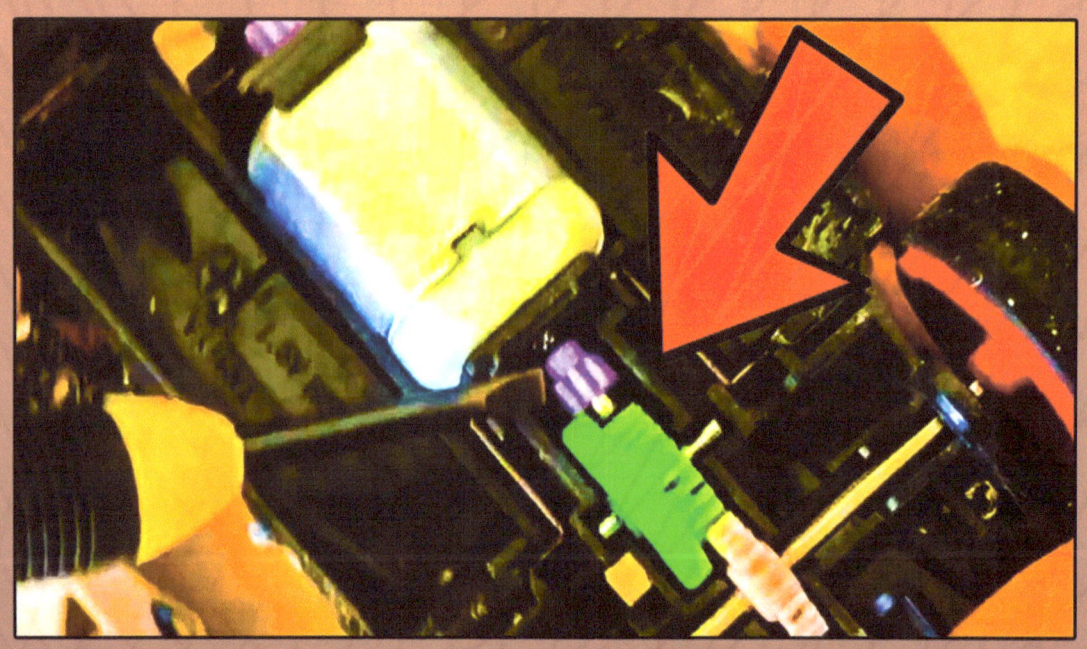

One issue that may arise is that the grip of the pinion gear on the motor shaft becomes loose and as the motor shaft spins, the pinion gear no longer spins therefore the counter gear no longer spins ultimately resulting in no energy being tranferred to the tires meaning that the car does not move forward.

The Motor Cover

For the Mid Motor (A) chassis, the motor and gears are secured by a slide-on cover which also acts as security for the batteries.

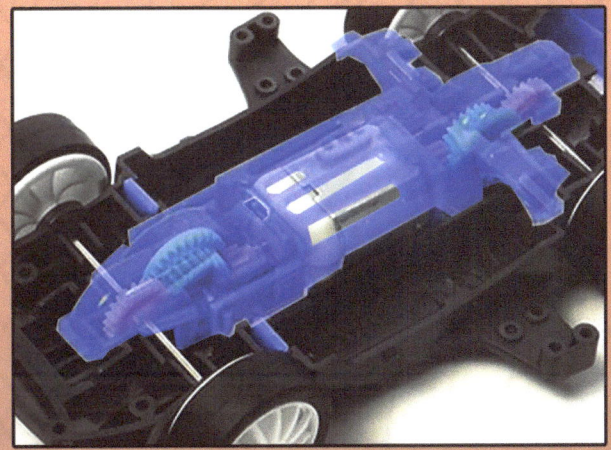 

Additially, the motor is secured to the chassis by a pair of mounts that are situated at the front and rear of the 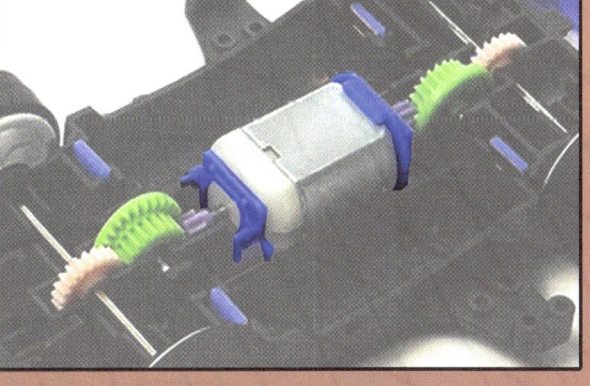 motor as shown in the image bottom right.

Those motor mounts clip into the chassis and are easily removed for swapping motors during pit stops.

12

The Transponder Mount
aka Brake and Inverted Brake

The Mid Motor (A) chassis is equipped with a single static braking mechanism that is intended to slow down the car on a sharp incline by making contact with the track surface.

For our purposes, we use the brake as the bottom plate for the transponder mount and other brake inverted for the top transponder mount plate with the use of aluminum spacers for creating the appropriate space for a snug and secure fit around the transponder.

The Spacers, Screws and Washers

For the transponder to be attached to the chassis, we need spacers, screws and washers as seen in the image.

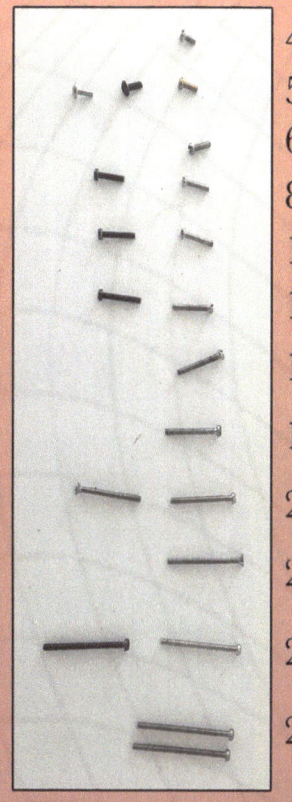

4mm
5mm
6mm
8mm
10mm
12mm
15mm
17mm
20mm
23mm
25mm
29mm

Screws and washers are also used to secure the rollers which we will discuss, later.

It is important to have a full set of spacers, screws and washers on hand for repairs.

ROUTE
66
Races

The Rollers

To keep the car from scrapping along the side walls of the track, horizontal roller discs are mounted on all four corners of the chassis.

Rollers are held on by screws and washers of which the screws are tightened by a right hand turn, whereby racing on a track in a clockwise direction may result in a loosened and lost roller.

Also, a seized up roller will become damaged due to friction with   the track wall.

The Plates

To prevent damage due to the soft nature of the chassis plastic, drivers may choose to add carbon plates to the front and/or rear of their car by attaching those plates to the existing chassis.

Even if there is already chassis damage, plates are able to be attached to what is left.

Also, in the image, you might notice that there are roller upgrades from plastic to ball bearing types.

ROUTE 66 Races

The Bodies

Although the car bodies last forever, some parts of the body may become damaged, such as the rear body spoiler and the front and rear latches which hold the body to the chassis.

Rear body spoilers and body latches are necessary to start and finish races because there are certain advantages and disadvantages, otherwise.

It is always a good idea to have a backup spoiler and body latches.

17

ROUTE
66
Races

The Weight and or Ballast

From the factory, each part may not end up weighing the same as identical other parts.

CHASSIS	BODY	DRY	BATTERY	WET
65.6g	9.1g	75.2g	52.3g	127.5g
65.4g	8.8g	74.6g	51.8g	126.4g
65.5g	9.0g	75.0g	52.2g	127.2g
65.4g	8.9g	74.9g	52.1g	127.0g
65.4g	8.8g	74.8g	52.0g	126.9g
65.4g	8.8g	74.7g	51.9g	126.6g
65.4g	8.8g	74.6g	51.8g	126.4g

Also, different car bodies will have different weights due to their differing designs.

If a car is having trouble staying on the track or staying within its class speed limit, extra weight can help and is sometimes required for qualifying.

18

ROUTE
66
Races

The Batteries

Each type of battery has its own characteristics.

For one, an Eneloop Pro battery is known for its overly tight fit into the battery compartment.

This may be an advantage for coninued flow of energy during rough racing conditions, however pit stops can take longer for extracating stuck batteries.

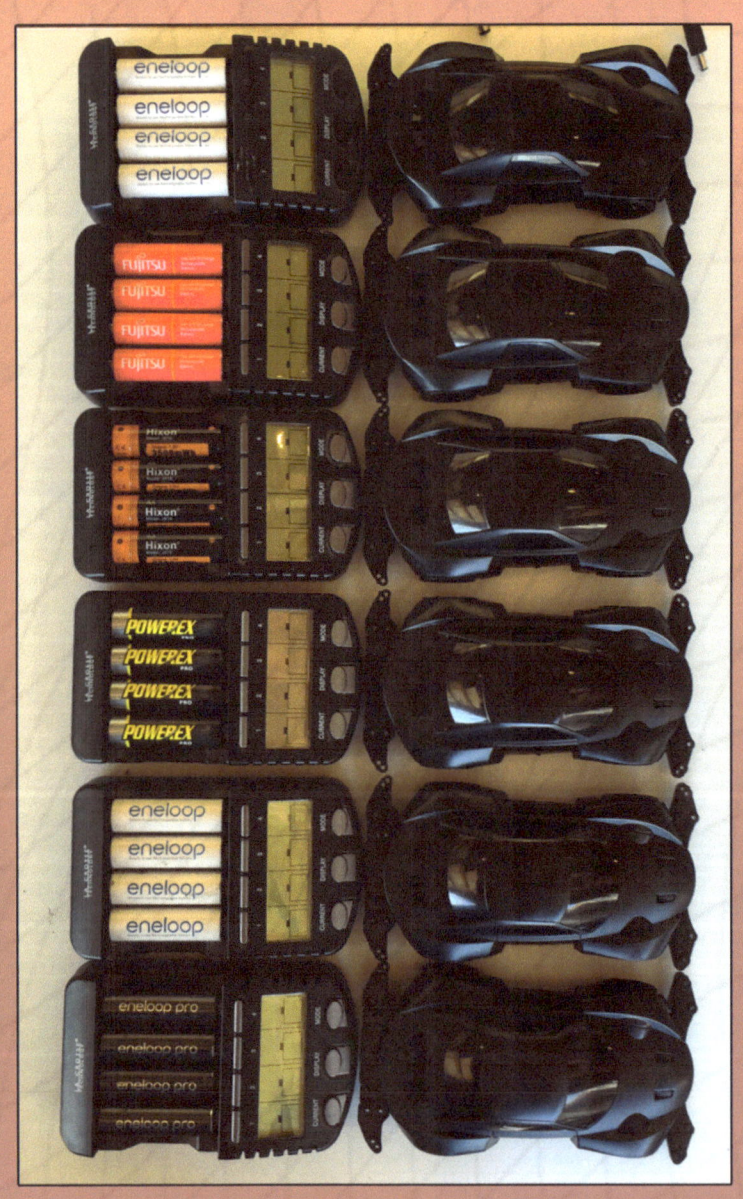

The Batteries (continued)

For speed classes using the Hixon 1.5V battery at 3500 mWh, (converts to like 3000mAh) those batteries require a different type of charger.

As seen in the photo, Hixon batteries do not register on the smaller, standard sized charger used for all of the other batteries.

ROUTE 66 Races

The Corner Scale

This is a quick way to figure out how the weight is distributed in your car or for the indiviudal parts.

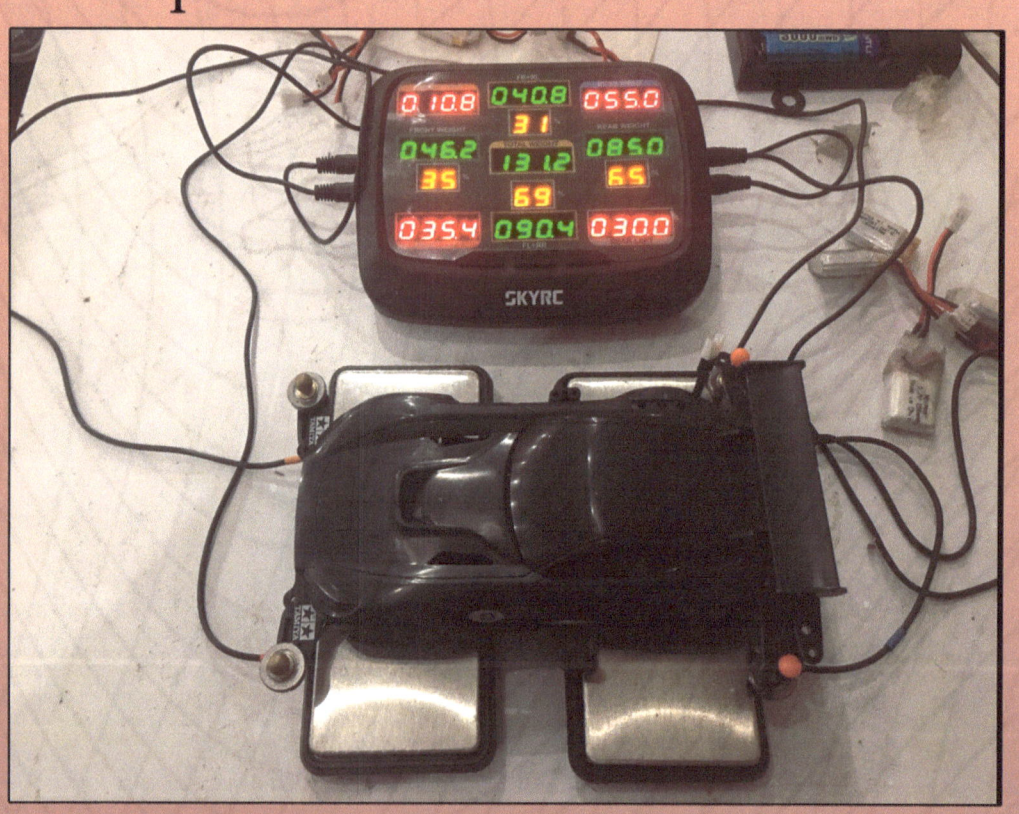

Take a car and place each tire onto a separate weight pad and see how much each corner weighs or take four (4) identical parts and see if any of them weigh more or less than the others.

The Pinion Gear Ratio

Each new car is equipped with a set of 8-tooth pinion gears which have a radius of 4.87mm.

8-tooth
4.87mm

10-tooth
5.75mm

9-tooth
5.36mm

11-tooth
6.35mm

Depending on the clearance with the counter gear, pinion gears with 6 to 10 teeth may be used to bring a car into the appropriate speed limit window for its class.

Considered an expert driver modification, pinion gear changes are not for everyone.

The Counter Gear Ratio

By combining a variety of pinion gear ratios with a variety of counter gear ratios, quite an array of ratios will be available.

GEAR RATIOS

T	C	S	R
6	Y	Y	5.78
6	G	G	5.51
7	Y	Y	4.95
7	G	G	4.72
8	Y	Y	4.33
8	G	G	4.13
9	Y	Y	4.04
8	B	0	4.00
8	Y	P	3.70
9	G	G	3.67
10	Y	Y	3.46
8	G	P	3.50
10	G	G	3.31

(ratios are approximate and should be verified)

23

The Ball Bearing Rollers

In the comparison between plastic and metal rollers, the ball bearing type of metal rollers are definitely going to provide much reduced friction allowing for higher speeds slightly offset by the added weight which could be a good thing.

In testing four (4) types of ball bearing rollers, all seemed to have similar performance, some have more tolerance for moisture and some more prone to seize up from track debris grit.

Still, metal ball bearing rollers are preferrred for their lower maintenence schedule.

The Motor RPM Range

Identical motors mostly do not have the same identical RPM's or revolutions per minute.

As stated on the specifications for each motor, there will be a range of RPM.

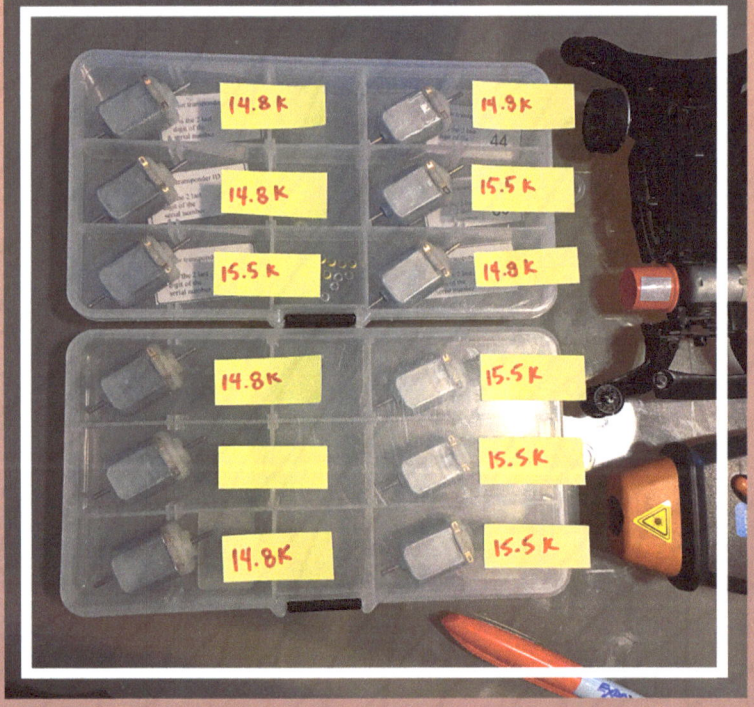

A typical Orange motor will have a variable RPM range of between 12,000 to 14,300.

Sometimes, motors are outside of their stated and expected low or high boundaries where having several motors and testing them could provide a driver with more stragetic motor usage to either increase or decrease the car's speed at crucial points of the race.

The Lights

The use of lights are allowed for day or night racing and add a bit of fun to the show.

Nock lights for archery work really well for this purpose as they are able to be mounted to the car with their own power source and not drain any energy from the car's battery.

For racing at night on a large track that may not have adequate lighting, lights would help marshals see if a car was stuck on the track or sitting somewhere off the track.

Of course, any stuck car would be noticed once it did not register on the lap monitor.

Route 66 Races is in association with

Route66Artists.com | Mini4WD.com | 66TheRoute.com

Route66Chess.com | Route66Savings.com | Route66Organic.com

Route66Family.com | Route66Friends.com | Route66Farms.com

Whoot66.com | Whoof66.com | 22Camels.com

If you are interested in building and hosting
a "Route 66 Races" race track or
if you are an artist interested in contributing
your Route 66 related artwork or lyrics,
please send a text to 949-424-6496
or email donutbookscom@gmail.com.

All contributing artists will be eligible
to receive 100% of the profits from their works
by being included, for printed merchandise,
in the Route 66 Artists catalog and website.

1926-2026

www.ingramcontent.com/pod-product-compliance
Lightning Source LLC
Chambersburg PA
CBHW041609120626

46551CB00002B/371